Original title:
Happiness Path

Author: Thor Castlebury
ISBN HARDBACK: 978-9916-88-148-4
ISBN PAPERBACK: 978-9916-88-149-1

Colors of the Heart

In the dawn, a soft hue shows,
Whispers of light on fragile rose.
Blushing moments, sweet and bright,
Painting dreams in morning light.

In twilight's glow, shadows play,
Crimson skies at end of day.
Silent wishes on the breeze,
Carried softly through the trees.

In midnight's calm, deep blue reigns,
Echoes of our quiet pains.
Stars like brush strokes grace the dark,
Guiding souls with gentle spark.

In every shade, our feelings blend,
A canvas where our hearts can mend.
Each color tells a tale unspoken,
The hues of love, never broken.

The Echo of Joy

In laughter's light, we find our way,
A melody that brightens the day.
With each small giggle, our hearts align,
A joyful song, in spirit divine.

Through valleys low and mountains high,
The echo of joy will never die.
In simple things, we find the bliss,
A fleeting moment, not to miss.

Paths Woven with Smiles

Along the trail where sunlight gleams,
We walk on paths of golden dreams.
Every step shared, with smiles so bright,
Guiding us through the soft twilight.

Threads of laughter we gently weave,
In this tapestry, we believe.
With open hearts, the journey we take,
Creating joy with each bond we make.

An Odyssey of Optimism

Across the seas of hope we sail,
Braving storms with a vibrant trail.
With every wave, our spirits rise,
In the horizon, a new sun flies.

Focusing on the light ahead,
In dreams of better, we are fed.
Together we stand, hand in hand,
An odyssey, forever planned.

The Flourish of Feelings

In gardens lush, our hearts do bloom,
With every petal, we dispel gloom.
Feelings dance like leaves in the breeze,
Creating memories, sweet to seize.

With roots of trust and branches wide,
In the flourish of feelings, we abide.
Let love's essence fill the air,
A vibrant world, beyond compare.

Joyful Journey

In the morning light we go,
With laughter bright and spirits glow.
Through fields of dreams and skies of blue,
Each step we take, a love so true.

With every path and winding road,
Our hearts keep time, a gentle code.
Together, hand in hand we roam,
This joyful journey feels like home.

Steps of Serenity

Soft whispers in the evening air,
Each gentle breath, a silent prayer.
Through tranquil woods where shadows play,
We find our peace at end of day.

The rustling leaves, a soothing song,
In every step, we feel we belong.
With nature's grace, our spirits rise,
In perfect calm, beneath the skies.

Radiance in Every Footfall

With every step, the world ignites,
A dance of joy in sunlit sights.
Each footfall leaves a sparkling trace,
A glow of love, a warm embrace.

As sunlight dapples on the ground,
In every heartbeat, magic found.
We walk in wonder, hearts so free,
Radiance shines in you and me.

The Trail of Light

In twilight's glow, our journey starts,
With twinkling stars, we play our parts.
The trail of light, so brightly cast,
Guides us forward, a spell so vast.

With every step, the shadows fade,
In golden beams, our fears allayed.
Together we will find our way,
On this trail, forever stay.

Sunshine on the Trail

Golden rays dance on leaves,
Footsteps tap on the ground.
Nature whispers sweet songs,
Joy in every sound.

Birds flutter high above,
A breeze carries their cheer.
With each step I take forward,
The world feels bright and near.

Laughter echoes through trees,
The path leads me away.
Sunshine warms my spirit,
Guiding me through the day.

Moments wrapped in the light,
A journey so divine.
In this place of wonder,
Every heartbeat is mine.

Cascades of Contentment

Water flows in gentle streams,
Soft shadows cast so wide.
Peaceful whispers fill the air,
Nature's loving guide.

Mountains stand with quiet grace,
Their peaks kissed by the sun.
In this tranquil setting,
Worry is undone.

Leaves rustle with the wind,
Nature's sweet embrace.
In the rhythm of the earth,
I find my special place.

Cascades sing their soft tune,
Clarity within reach.
Contentment flows like rivers,
In silence, I find peace.

The Glow of Each Step

With each step, I feel the spark,
A light guiding my way.
Through shadows and through twilight,
Hope's glow will never sway.

The path beneath my feet is bright,
Illuminated and clear.
Each moment shines with purpose,
As I move without fear.

Stars above begin to glow,
Their dance a wondrous sight.
In the quiet of the night,
I find my heart's delight.

The journey brings me closer,
To dreams that gently crept.
With every step I take tonight,
My soul's warmth is kept.

Seasons of Smiles

Spring brings blooms of bright colors,
Laughter fills the air.
Each moment shared with loved ones,
Happiness we wear.

Summer's sun plays on our skin,
Days filled with golden rays.
Memories made in warm embraces,
Time's sweet, gentle ways.

Autumn shows its palette bold,
Leaves fall like whispered dreams.
Together in the crisp cool air,
Joy is here, it seems.

Winter wraps us close in white,
Soft snowflakes gently fall.
The warmth of hearts ignites the cold,
In love, we find it all.

Breezes of Kindness

In the quiet dawn, they flow,
Gentle whispers, soft and slow.
Carrying warmth, a sweet embrace,
Touching hearts in every place.

Like petals falling from the trees,
They dance upon the summer breeze.
Each act blooms, a fragrant sign,
In this world, kindness intertwines.

A smile shared, a helping hand,
Small gestures spread across the land.
Together we can start to see,
The beauty found in you and me.

Let kindness spread, a woven thread,
Binding souls with love instead.
With every breeze that comes our way,
Let kindness guide us every day.

Revel in the Radiance

Beneath the sun, we lift our gaze,
Eyes alight with golden rays.
In every laugh, in every cheer,
The radiance of joy draws near.

Like starlit nights that warmly glow,
The light within helps us to grow.
In every moment, let us bask,
In the glow of love—no greater task.

Dance to the rhythm, feel it rise,
With radiant hearts, we touch the skies.
In every heartbeat, every sigh,
Revel in the light, let spirits fly.

With hues of dawn and dusk entwined,
In this vibrant world, our dreams aligned.
Embrace the warmth, let worries fade,
In the radiance, memories made.

Footprints on Cloud Nine

The skies are blue, our hearts take flight,
We wander softly, pure delight.
With every step on softest air,
We leave our whispers everywhere.

In laughter shared, we find our way,
Through dreamlike realms where shadows play.
Each footprint light, each moment bright,
On cloud nine, we dance in light.

Like gentle rain on thirsty ground,
Our joys and hopes are all around.
In this realm where love is fine,
We trace our steps on cloud nine.

Through every turn, new paths unfold,
In the warmth of dreams, we're bold.
With every heartbeat, hearts aligned,
We leave sweet footprints, intertwined.

Lanterns of Laughter

In the darkness, light a flame,
With every chuckle, call a name.
Lanterns flicker, casting cheer,
In joyous moments, we draw near.

With laughter shared, our spirits soar,
Like open hearts, we then explore.
Each giggle brightens the night sky,
Illuminating dreams nearby.

Through whispered tales and silly games,
Our laughter echoes, never tames.
In every heart a lantern glows,
Burning brightly, love bestows.

So gather round, let spirits sing,
In every jest, the joy we bring.
Together we light the darkened scenes,
With lanterns of laughter, pure and keen.

The Road to Radiance

In the dawn's golden light,
Shadows dance away,
Paths ahead beckon bright,
Hope guides the way.

Every step ignites dreams,
Wisps of joy in the air,
Whispers soft as moonbeams,
Life quivers with care.

Through valleys of strife,
And mountains of fear,
Each heartbeat is life,
The spirit draws near.

Onward I shall tread,
With courage, I soar,
Embracing what's spread,
A future in store.

The Colors of Elation

In fields where flowers bloom,
Colors dance and sway,
Every petal, a tune,
That brightens the day.

Sunset paints the skies,
With shades both warm and bold,
In laughter, life lies,
A canvas of gold.

Joy splashes the scene,
A palette so vast,
In moments serene,
The present holds fast.

With each hue, I feel,
The rhythm of zest,
Life's vibrant reveal,
In colors, I rest.

Moments of Ecstasy

In the heartbeat of night,
Stars glimmer above,
Every whisper feels right,
Wrapped in pure love.

Time pauses its stroll,
As laughter takes flight,
In this joyous role,
We lose track of night.

With every glance shared,
Magic fills the air,
Hearts open, ensnared,
In moments so rare.

Together we sway,
In a dreamlike trance,
Lost in the array,
Of life's sweet romance.

A Voyage of Smiles

On a ship made of dreams,
We sail the wide sea,
With laughter that gleams,
A journey set free.

Waves whisper to play,
In the sun's warm embrace,
Each moment, a sway,
Time holds a soft grace.

Through horizons we roam,
Chasing joy's bright flame,
In smiles, we find home,
Life whispers our name.

Together we'll glide,
With the winds as our song,
In this love, we bide,
Where we both belong.

Embracing Elation

In the glow of morning light,
Happiness takes its flight.
With laughter in the air,
Joy dances everywhere.

Colors bright, a vivid scene,
Life is pure, and hearts are keen.
Share a smile, spread the cheer,
Embrace the warmth, hold it dear.

Moments passed, yet they remain,
Cascading like a gentle rain.
In this bliss, we find our place,
United in a warm embrace.

So let's sing, and shout aloud,
In our hearts, we stand so proud.
Embracing all the gifts we find,
In elation, hearts aligned.

Meadow of Merriment

In a meadow lush and wide,
Laughter comes like a joyful tide.
Breezes soft, the sun so bright,
Hearts take wing, reaching new height.

Fluttering flowers, colors soar,
Each petal whispers tales of lore.
Children play, their spirits high,
As butterflies flit through the sky.

Beneath the trees, we gather near,
In this haven, we shed each fear.
With every gaze, our spirits lift,
Moments shared, the greatest gift.

Let's run barefoot on this ground,
In the laughter, joy is found.
In this meadow, forever stay,
A sanctuary where hearts play.

The Tapestry of Joy

Threads of laughter weave so bright,
Stories shared in soft moonlight.
Each moment stitched, a vibrant hue,
Together we create anew.

Memories dance, patterns form,
In this tapestry, hearts stay warm.
Every joy, a precious thread,
Binding us, where love is spread.

With every knot, we find our way,
In life's fabric, come what may.
Strength in unity, side by side,
In this art, our hearts abide.

So let us weave with gentle care,
A tapestry that we all share.
In every stitch, our spirits rise,
A masterpiece beneath the skies.

Portraits of a Grateful Heart

In the canvas painted bright,
Gratitude glows, a pure delight.
Every stroke, a story told,
In vibrant shades, our hearts unfold.

Moments cherished, memories dear,
With each brush, we hold them near.
From simple joys to grand displays,
Our grateful heart forever stays.

Through twilight's calm and dawn's embrace,
These portraits capture time and space.
In every glance, a glimpse of grace,
A reminder of love's warm trace.

So let us paint with colors bold,
In grateful hearts, true treasures unfold.
With every masterpiece we create,
A legacy of love innate.

Glimmers of Joy

In the morning light, we find,
Soft whispers of hope unwind.
Hearts dance with a quiet cheer,
As dreams awaken, drawing near.

Through the shadows, warmth does gleam,
Each moment a fleeting dream.
With laughter wrapped in golden rays,
We cherish these simple days.

The world paints colors bright and bold,
In tales of joy, we are told.
Together we journey, hand in hand,
In this vibrant, loving land.

With every smile, a spark ignites,
In the tapestry of our nights.
Glimmers of joy forever flow,
In the heart's embrace, we grow.

Beyond the Meadows

Fields of green stretch far and wide,
Where quiet streams and secrets bide.
Butterflies dance in sunlight's glow,
As gentle breezes softly blow.

The hills rise high with stories old,
Their whispers weave a fabric bold.
In every corner, life abounds,
With magic in the softest sounds.

Walking paths where wildflowers bloom,
Nature's brush erases gloom.
Underneath the azure sky,
In every heart, a yearning sigh.

Beyond the meadows, dreams take flight,
In endless realms of purest light.
We wander forth with hope in sight,
Embracing all that feels so right.

Echoes of Laughter

In the corners of our mind,
Echoes of laughter intertwined.
Memories dance like leaves in air,
With every chuckle, love we share.

Joyful moments, brief yet bright,
Illuminating darkest night.
With friends beside, we climb so high,
Reaching stars while spirits fly.

In a world where worries cease,
Laughter brings a sense of peace.
Together we weave a tale so sweet,
In every heartbeat, life's true beat.

May echoes linger, ever clear,
Through trials faced, we persevere.
In each smile, may warmth ignite,
As laughter leads us to the light.

The Sunshine Trail

On a path where shadows fade,
The sunshine trail begins to wade.
With every step, the heart takes flight,
In the warm embrace of golden light.

Nature's symphony plays sweet notes,
Guiding us with gentle quotes.
Breezes whisper through the leaves,
In the warmth, the spirit believes.

Gathering hope like stars at dusk,
We travel forth, in dreams we trust.
Hand in hand, we face the day,
On the sunshine trail, we find our way.

Every moment, a gift to hold,
As stories of our lives unfold.
Together we walk, forever free,
On this trail of joy, you and me.

The Lantern of Laughter

In the night, a flicker bright,
Echoes of joy take flight.
Whispers dance on the breeze,
Laughter wraps us like trees.

A glow that warms the soul,
In every heart, it makes us whole.
Lighting paths through shadowed fears,
A beacon that wipes away tears.

Jokes and stories fill the air,
Moments shared with laughter rare.
Around the fire, friends unite,
In the lantern's loving light.

Each chuckle a spark of joy,
A tender gift, not just a toy.
With laughter, we learn to soar,
The lantern burns forevermore.

Radiance in Motion

The sun kisses the breaking dawn,
Colors swirl as night is gone.
Nature wakes, in vibrant hues,
Life dances in morning's muse.

Branches sway, a gentle sigh,
Birds take flight across the sky.
Every leaf in golden glow,
Shows the world how beauty flows.

Footsteps lead on winding trails,
Through the woods, as the heart fails.
Yet radiance guides our way,
In every moment, bright and gay.

Skies embrace the sunlit day,
In motion, the warmth will stay.
Each breath whispers, 'Feel the light,'
As joy and peace take gentle flight.

Journeys Bathed in Sunlight

On the road where shadows fade,
Sunlight beams, the path is laid.
Every step, a new delight,
In the warmth, our spirits ignite.

Winding trails, the trees applaud,
Nature's canvas, a bright façade.
With each mile, our burdens lift,
In sunlight's glow, a treasured gift.

Adventures waiting all around,
In laughter's echo, joy is found.
With open hearts, we roam anew,
Journeys bright, a vibrant view.

As golden rays embrace the land,
Together we will always stand.
In sunlight's glow, our spirits soar,
Creating memories that restore.

Treasures of Cheerfulness

In the garden, blooms arise,
Colors burst, a sweet surprise.
Each petal holds a secret cheer,
A treasure found, so bright and clear.

Laughter rings like chimes so sweet,
With every smile, our hearts repeat.
Gathered moments, rich and rare,
Wrapped in joy beyond compare.

With friends beside, we share the light,
Through every challenge, hearts take flight.
In every glance, a spark ignites,
Cheerfulness, our daily rites.

Living life in vibrant hues,
We chase the sun, ignore the blues.
In every heart, a treasure chest,
Of cheerfulness, we are blessed.

Walking on Sunshine

Bright rays dance on my skin,
The world feels alive within.
Every step a joyful beat,
In this warmth, my heart's complete.

Laughter echoes in the air,
With every moment, I declare.
Life's a gift, no need to frown,
As I wander through this town.

Colors burst around my eyes,
Underneath the endless skies.
With each breath, I find my place,
In this vibrant, warm embrace.

Walking forward, worries cease,
In this light, I find my peace.
With each stride, my spirit soars,
Walking on sunshine, I want more.

The Breeze of Bliss

Gentle winds that softly sigh,
Whisper secrets passing by.
In their arms, I feel so free,
Carried far to where I'll be.

Leaves are dancing, swaying light,
Underneath the starry night.
Every breath, a soothing prayer,
In the breeze, I shed my care.

Moments fleeting, time stands still,
Wrapped in joy, I feel the thrill.
Nature calls, a sweet embrace,
In this flow, I find my space.

Breeze of bliss, you lift my soul,
With your touch, I become whole.
In your presence, life's a song,
With you here, I know I belong.

The Narrative of Joy

Pages filled with tales of cheer,
Every laugh, the world draws near.
Stories shared from heart to heart,
In this dance, we play our part.

Chapters turn with every smile,
Life's a journey, mile by mile.
In the moments, we create,
Future bright, it's not too late.

With each word, a spark ignites,
Filling days with pure delights.
In the rhythm, life flows free,
Writing our own history.

Narrative of joy unfolds,
In the warmth, the magic holds.
Together we shall write and play,
In this story, come what may.

The Quest for Elation

Through valleys deep and mountains high,
Seeking joy beneath the sky.
With a heart that yearns for more,
On this quest, I'll boldly soar.

Footsteps echo on the ground,
In the silence, peace is found.
Each adventure whispers near,
Guiding me to what is dear.

In the laughter and the tears,
In the shadows of my fears.
Elation waits beyond the bend,
With each step, I find a friend.

The quest continues, never done,
In the journey, life's a run.
Chasing dreams that light the way,
Elation blooms with every day.

Steps Towards the Sky

With open hearts, we dare to rise,
Reaching out to touch the skies.
Each step we take, a dream unfolds,
Adventure waits, the brave and bold.

Clouds may gather, winds may blow,
But faith within will help us grow.
Mountains climbed with strength anew,
Together we will see it through.

The horizon beckons, bright and far,
With every challenge, we will spar.
Steps forward lead to skies so wide,
In unity, we shall abide.

Ribbons of Radiance

A tapestry of colors bright,
Woven together, pure delight.
Threads of laughter, strands of grace,
In every heart, a sacred space.

Ribbons dance in morning light,
Whispering hopes, a joyful sight.
Through storms they weave, unfurl, and sway,
Guiding us along the way.

In the glow of a setting sun,
Together, we have just begun.
With every ribbon, every hue,
Radiance flows, forever true.

The Lightness of Being

In the soft glow of dawn,
Life whispering gentle dreams.
Wings unfurl in the quiet,
Floating on sunlight beams.

Each moment a fleeting dance,
Soft laughter escapes the heart.
In the stillness, we find peace,
Where worries and burdens part.

Clouds drift lazily above,
Every breath a sweet release.
In the canvas of the sky,
We paint our souls with ease.

With joy wrapped in silence,
We rise, unshackled, free.
In the lightness of being,
We become what we can be.

Trails of Tranquility

Amidst the whispering trees,
Soft breezes carry the day.
Paths woven through verdant fields,
Nature's embrace leads the way.

Gentle streams hum a song,
Each ripple sparks soothing cheer.
In the heart of the moment,
The world fades, calm and clear.

Clouds drape the horizon low,
Painting shadows on the land.
In each footstep, we wander,
Finding peace, hand in hand.

The sun dips low and sighs,
As stars begin their soft flight.
In trails of tranquility,
We walk into the night.

Embracing Every Smile

A laugh dances in the air,
Brightening the dullest days.
In the warmth of a kind glance,
Hope rises in myriad ways.

Each smile, a spark of light,
Illuminating the path.
In the tapestry of moments,
We weave joy, love, and wrath.

Hearts open wide like flowers,
Blooming under the sun's grace.
In every shared connection,
We find home in each face.

With arms outstretched in trust,
We embrace both joy and strife.
In the cadence of laughter,
We celebrate this gift of life.

The Expedition of Euphoria

Footsteps echo in the vast,
Fields of dreams begin to call.
With spirits high and eyes bright,
We journey, ready for it all.

Every turn reveals a path,
Filled with wonders yet unseen.
Adventure waits in the heart,
In moments crisp and serene.

The mountains rise like whispers,
Challenges carved from stone.
Through trials, we find our strength,
Together, never alone.

As horizons stretch before us,
The sky bursts with vibrant hue.
In the expedition of euphoria,
The world blooms fresh and new.

Dancing on the Breeze

Gentle whispers through the trees,
Leaves that flutter, dance with ease.
Sunlight glimmers on the ground,
Nature's rhythm all around.

Barefoot steps on grass so bright,
Carried dreams take joyful flight.
Moments cherished, hearts set free,
In the dance of harmony.

Windswept laughter fills the air,
Each soft smile, a hidden prayer.
Together twirling, spirits soar,
In this world, who could ask for more?

Echoes fade as daylight wanes,
Still we sway, forgetting pains.
In the dusk, with stars we tease,
Forever dancing on the breeze.

Trails of Warmth

Paths that weave through golden fields,
Every step, a joy that yields.
Sunbeams kissing earth so sweet,
Nature's heartbeat, light on feet.

Winding trails invite the soul,
Where the whispers make us whole.
Each new twist, a hidden gem,
As we journey through the hem.

Gathered warmth from hands we hold,
Stories shared and dreams retold.
Footprints marked in soft brown clay,
Memories linger, here to stay.

In the distance, shadows fall,
Yet in our hearts, we stand so tall.
Forever grateful for the paths,
On these trails, life's gentle laughs.

The Blissful Expedition

Bags are packed, the journey calls,
Wanderlust within enthralls.
Every corner holds a thrill,
Adventure waits beyond the hill.

Sunrise paints the road ahead,
In our hearts, bright hopes are spread.
New horizons, skies so wide,
Together, we will take the ride.

With each step, we learn and grow,
Mingling with the ebb and flow.
Memories made, treasures found,
In laughter's echoes, joy is crowned.

The path unfolds, a gift each day,
In blissful bliss, we find our way.
For in this quest, we truly see,
The essence of exploration, wild and free.

Joy's Expansive Horizon

Gaze beyond the hills that rise,
Underneath the endless skies.
Promises in every hue,
Joy awakens, bright and new.

Boundless dreams that dance in light,
Hopeful hearts, a perfect sight.
Together we will chase the sun,
On this journey, we are one.

Laughter echoes through the day,
In each moment, come what may.
Through the shadows, we will gleam,
Life's a canvas, paint the dream.

With each breath, the world expands,
Open hearts, we make our plans.
For joy is not a distant trace,
It's here and now, our sacred space.

The Essence of Elation

In the morning light we rise,
With laughter dancing in our eyes.
Every moment feels so bright,
A celebration of pure delight.

Joy flows like a gentle stream,
In every heartbeat, every dream.
We hold the world in our embrace,
Finding magic in every place.

With friends beside us, hand in hand,
Together we can surely stand.
The essence of our happiness,
Lies in love, we must confess.

Let every smile pave the way,
To cherish life in every sway.
Elation's song we'll always sing,
In the heart, it's everything.

Mosaic of Merriment

Colors bright upon the wall,
Each tile represents us all.
In laughter's hue, we find our part,
Creating art from every heart.

Joyful moments strung in line,
In woven tales, our spirits shine.
Fragments of our lives so sweet,
A mosaic where souls can meet.

Dance and twirl within the light,
In shared stories, pure delight.
Each smile adds a brilliant shade,
In this tapestry we've made.

Together we will paint the night,
With stars above, our dreams in flight.
A mosaic of merriment anew,
In every moment, me and you.

The Soothing Pathway

Beneath the trees, the shadows play,
A gentle breeze along the way.
With every step, we find our peace,
In nature's arms, our worries cease.

The rustling leaves, a soothing sound,
In the whispering woods, we are found.
With each breath, the world grows still,
A quiet calm, a tranquil thrill.

Sunlight dances through the trees,
Painting patterns on the breeze.
Each pathway leads to hidden dreams,
Where hope flows softly, like sunbeams.

Hand in hand, we walk along,
To the rhythm of nature's song.
On this soothing path we roam,
In the heart, we've found our home.

Celebrations in Every Step

With every stride, a reason to cheer,
In every heartbeat, life draws near.
Joy unfolds in moments small,
Celebrations echo, bright and tall.

Through each sunrise, new hopes arise,
In every gaze, the spark defies.
Life's little wins, we hold them tight,
Celebrations glow in morning light.

Together we march, united and strong,
In rhythm with time, we all belong.
Every journey's filled with zest,
Celebrations in our very quest.

Let's dance through life, both brave and free,
Embrace each moment, just you and me.
With laughter as our guiding map,
Celebrations fill the world's vast gap.

Whispers of Delight

In the garden, petals sway,
Secrets shared in soft display.
Gentle hues of morning light,
Dance around, pure souls in flight.

Every laugh, a sweet embrace,
Moments cherished, time can't erase.
In the breeze, the whispers call,
Echoing joy, uniting all.

Nature hums a tranquil tune,
Softly cradling dreams by noon.
Underneath the branches wide,
Hearts find peace, love as their guide.

With each sound, the world stands still,
In this hush, we feel the thrill.
Whispers linger, soft and bright,
Filling shadows with delight.

A Walk Through Sunshine

Step by step on golden paths,
Sunshine chuckles, gently laughs.
Warmth envelops, hearts combine,
Fingers trace the sun's design.

Blossoms sway with every breeze,
Nature's joy, a tranquil tease.
Chasing beams of radiant light,
In this warmth, our spirits ignite.

Footprints marked on dusty trails,
Echo of the laughter prevails.
Each moment, a story spun,
Together, our journey has begun.

The world glows in vibrant hues,
In this dance, we cannot lose.
A walk through sunshine, hand in hand,
A symphony that's simply grand.

Echoes of Euphoria

In the valleys, laughter rings,
Joyful moments, graceful flings.
Hearts beat wild like drums in time,
Life's sweet notes, a perfect rhyme.

Dancing shadows, bright and free,
Whispers flow like melody.
Each echo carries joy and zest,
In our world, we feel refreshed.

Through valleys deep and mountains tall,
Euphoria invites us all.
Harmonies of love resound,
In our souls, pure bliss is found.

With every breath, the magic grows,
In every smile, the spirit glows.
Echoes of laughter in the air,
Binding us in dreams we share.

The Road to Bliss

Along the path where flowers bloom,
A journey unfolds, dispelling gloom.
Each step taken, joy ignites,
Guiding hearts to heights of light.

To the mountains, through the trees,
Whispers carried by the breeze.
Every moment, pure embrace,
The road to bliss, our sacred place.

Stars above, a guiding sight,
In the darkness, love shines bright.
Hand in hand, we walk as one,
Chasing sunsets 'til day is done.

With laughter soft and echoes clear,
Memories woven, held so dear.
The road to bliss, forever near,
In every heart, it's crystal clear.

Glows of Gratitude

In the quiet morn's embrace,
Sunrise paints a gentle glow,
Whispers of love in the air,
Gratitude seeds begin to grow.

Each moment blooms like spring's flower,
Brightening paths where shadows lay,
Hearts open in the light's power,
Thankfulness fills the day.

Through trials faced and lessons learned,
Life's beauty shines in every tear,
In every corner, joy discerned,
Gratitude holds us ever near.

Together we cherish each gift,
Building bonds that brightly last,
In the glow of hearts that lift,
Memories rich, forever cast.

The Serene Sojourn

Upon the hill at twilight's call,
A tranquil breeze, the evening's song,
Nature's peace begins to sprawl,
In this stillness, I belong.

Stars awaken in skies so wide,
Filling darkness with their light,
Each moment, a gentle ride,
On waves of calm, a soft delight.

The world slows to a tender hum,
As thoughts drift like clouds up high,
In the stillness, whispers come,
Of dreams that in silence lie.

With every breath, the heart can find,
A sanctuary, pure and true,
In this serene sojourn, I unwind,
Embracing peace, renewing you.

Steps Towards Wonder

In fields of green where daisies sway,
Each step taken leads to more,
With open eyes, I seize the day,
Wonder waiting to explore.

The flutter of a butterfly,
A child's laughter fills the air,
Every moment passes by,
Revealing treasures, bright and rare.

With every footfall, magic glows,
In simple things, true joy is found,
Through meadows wild, my spirit flows,
In every corner, life astounds.

As stars emerge and night unfolds,
The universe sings soft and clear,
In every step, a story told,
Awakening the wonder near.

The Symphony of Joy

Notes of laughter fill the air,
Harmony of hearts entwined,
In every rhythm, love to share,
Life's great music, a joyful bind.

Dancing through both joy and strife,
Each melody a sacred gift,
In the symphony of life,
Together we find our spirits lift.

With every beat, a story sung,
Of friendship formed and dreams that thrive,
In vibrant colors, we are young,
With every note, we feel alive.

Let the echoes fill the night,
In this concert, souls unite,
Together, we sing, hearts in flight,
Creating a tapestry of light.

The Brightest Steps

With every dawn, a chance to rise,
We take the road where sunlight lies.
Each step we make, a dance of glee,
Our hearts ignite, we feel so free.

In laughter's echo, joy can bloom,
We chase the light, dispel the gloom.
Together strong, we pave the way,
In vibrant hues, we'll greet the day.

Through trials faced, our spirits grow,
In unity, we let love flow.
The brightest steps we boldly choose,
With every stride, we cannot lose.

Whispers of Cheer

In gentle tones, a song arises,
Whispers soft, a world surprises.
With arms outstretched, we share our hearts,
In simple acts, true love imparts.

A smile exchanged, a nod, a grin,
In little moments, we begin.
Through trials shared, our spirits lift,
Together, we create a gift.

With every word, a spark ignites,
Whispers of cheer on starry nights.
In kindness sewn, our dreams align,
We walk this path, your hand in mine.

Radiant Roadways

On radiant roadways, our feet we place,
With hopes that soar, we quicken the pace.
Through valleys low and mountains high,
Together, we touch the endless sky.

The shimmering path beneath our stride,
In every heart, we feel the pride.
With every step, we find our way,
In unity, we seize the day.

No shadow casts upon our dream,
In light we dance, a joyful beam.
The radiant road that we now claim,
Together we'll write our own sweet name.

The Pursuit of Bliss

In the pursuit of bliss, we roam,
Through open fields and skies our home.
With every breath, we chase the light,
In dreams afire, we take our flight.

With laughter's song, in joyous air,
We find our peace, let go of care.
Through winding paths where wildflowers play,
We share our hearts, come what may.

In quiet wishes and hopeful dreams,
Life unfolds in gentle streams.
To seek the bliss, we hold so dear,
With love as our guide, we have no fear.

Luminous Life

In the dawn's embrace, we rise anew,
Each ray a promise, bright and true.
Stars in our eyes, we chase the light,
In the tapestry of day, we find our might.

Nature's whispers, soft and kind,
In every shadow, treasures we find.
Life's vivid palette, colors ablaze,
In the art of living, we spend our days.

Moments captured, like fireflies' glow,
In the garden of time, let love overflow.
Laughter and tears, they dance in sync,
In the luminous life, we pause and think.

Heartbeats of Hope

A whispering breeze, the softest sigh,
In each heartbeat, our dreams will fly.
Amidst the chaos, we find our way,
In the rhythm of life, we learn to stay.

Hope like a flame, flickers within,
Casting shadows where love has been.
Through storms we wander, hand in hand,
In the heartbeats of hope, together we stand.

Promises linger, like stars in the night,
Guiding our paths, igniting our fight.
With courage as armor, we carry the load,
In each heartbeat of hope, love is bestowed.

Joyful Journey

On winding roads, we laugh and sing,
Each step we take, a joyful fling.
With open hearts, we embrace the skies,
Together we soar, a sweet surprise.

Mountains to climb, rivers to cross,
In every adventure, we gain, not loss.
Memories woven, with threads of gold,
In the joyful journey, our stories unfold.

Beneath the sun and the silver moon,
Life's perfect rhythm, a lovely tune.
Hand in hand, we savor the ride,
In the joyful journey, love is our guide.

Trails of Delight

Through forests deep, where shadows play,
We wander freely, come what may.
With laughter echoing, and hopes in flight,
On these trails of delight, hearts burn bright.

Butterflies dance in the warm sunlight,
Each moment cherished, each breath feels right.
In fields of dreams, we skip and sway,
On the trails of delight, we find our way.

The beauty of life, in petals and leaves,
In every heartbeat, the magic believes.
As we journey onward, side by side,
On the trails of delight, love is our guide.

Serendipitous Sojourn

Beneath the starlit sky, we roam,
Finding treasures in the unknown.
Whispers of fate guide our way,
In this journey, come what may.

Footsteps light on paths unseen,
Every corner holds a dream.
Moments stolen, laughter shared,
In fleeting time, we are ensnared.

With every turn, the heart expands,
A dance of life, in gentle hands.
Magic lingers in the air,
In serendipity, we're laid bare.

As dawn unfolds, we greet the light,
In the sojourn, everything feels right.
Forever changed, we take our stance,
In this beautiful, guided chance.

Pathways of Peace

Winding trails through towering trees,
Gentle whispers ride the breeze.
Footsteps soft on mossy ground,
In this haven, peace is found.

Sunlight dances on the stream,
Nature's pulse, a soothing dream.
Every breath, a calming note,
In this stillness, hearts will float.

Bridges built with hands held tight,
Sharing moments, pure delight.
In the silence, love will grow,
On pathways where the wildflowers glow.

Together here, our spirits soar,
In this peace, we find much more.
Echoes of joy in every space,
On these pathways, we embrace.

Gardens of Gratitude

In gardens lush, we sow our seeds,
With every bloom, our spirit feeds.
Petals soft in morning light,
Whispers of thanks, pure and bright.

Colors dance in vibrant hues,
In this haven, we choose to muse.
With every fragrance in the air,
Gratitude blooms, beyond compare.

Together we tend, hand in hand,
Planting hope across the land.
Every harvest, a shared delight,
In gardens of gratitude, our hearts ignite.

Seasons change, yet still we grow,
In this space, love's roots will show.
From every petal, joy will rise,
In gardens of gratitude, we find our skies.

The Symphony of Smiles

In a world where laughter flows,
The symphony of smiles glows.
Every grin a melody,
In this harmony, we're free.

Strings of joy play in our hearts,
A cadence where the magic starts.
With every note, our worries fade,
In this music, love is made.

Rhythms shared, a dance so sweet,
In connection, life's complete.
Echoes of joy in every face,
In this symphony, we find grace.

Through the highs and all the lows,
The symphony of smiles grows.
In every moment, purest bliss,
Embrace the song, we can't miss.

The Canvas of Contentment

Brush strokes of joy on the canvas wide,
Colors blend softly, no fear to hide.
A gentle smile echoes in each hue,
Peaceful moments, a dream come true.

Whispers of laughter, a melody sweet,
Beneath the sun's warmth, life feels complete.
Nature's embrace, a comforting hand,
In this vast world, together we stand.

Quiet reflections float on the breeze,
Among rustling leaves, hearts find their ease.
With every heartbeat, colors ignite,
The canvas of contentment, pure delight.

In the soft twilight, hues start to blend,
A sense of belonging, no need to pretend.
In each gentle stroke, love's light remains,
The canvas eternal, where joy sustains.

The Dance of Delight

Feet that twirl in the golden light,
Spinning and swaying, a wondrous sight.
Rhythms of laughter fill the air,
In the dance of delight, we shed our care.

With every leap, our spirits soar,
Lost in the moment, wanting more.
The world slows down with a merry cheer,
In the dance of delight, we know no fear.

Twinkling eyes ignite the night,
Together we move, hearts feeling light.
Joyful whispers surround us near,
In the dance of delight, life feels clear.

As the moon smiles down from above,
We twirl through the darkness, wrapped in love.
With every step, our passions unite,
In the endless rhythm, purest delight.

The Serenity Cycle

Morning light breaks with a soothing grace,
Nature awakens, filling the space.
Birdsong resounds in the fresh, cool air,
In the serenity cycle, nothing compares.

The sun climbs high, casting warm rays,
A gentle reminder of beautiful days.
Time flows softly like a quiet stream,
In the serenity cycle, we find our dream.

As twilight descends on the busy world,
Stars appear, shimmering, unfurled.
The moon whispers secrets of peace divine,
In the serenity cycle, all hearts align.

Night wraps around us, calm and deep,
In this sacred silence, we tenderly keep.
With every heartbeat, life starts anew,
In the serenity cycle, love carries through.

Trails of Tranquility

Winding paths through the emerald trees,
Each step forward brings a gentle ease.
Whispers of nature in every breeze,
On the trails of tranquility, the heart finds peace.

Pebbles crunch softly beneath our feet,
The beauty around us feels so complete.
In the presence of stillness, worries fade,
On the trails of tranquility, memories are made.

Sunlit clearings bring joy to our souls,
Hidden wonders that nature holds.
With every breath, harmony flows,
On the trails of tranquility, calmness grows.

As day turns to night, the stars appear,
Guiding our journey, ever near.
In nature's embrace, we truly find,
On the trails of tranquility, peace entwined.

Pathways of Positivity

We tread upon bright avenues,
Where hopes and dreams align.
Each step a joyful rhythm,
In the dance of life, we shine.

The sun spills gold on our journey,
Casting shadows far behind.
With courage, we keep moving,
In the heart, joy is defined.

With every smile exchanged,
The world becomes a glow.
Together, we lift each other,
Onward, love's ember will flow.

So let us walk in kindness,
As we face what lies ahead.
A pathway filled with promise,
Where all our hearts will tread.

The Garden of Gleeful Moments

Within this vibrant garden,
Blossoms of laughter grow.
Petals catch the sunlight,
With colors all aglow.

Each memory, a flower,
In sweet fragrance, they sway.
We cherish every heartbeat,
In this lively ballet.

The bees hum happy tunes,
While butterflies take flight.
In this sanctuary of joy,
We find our pure delight.

So let us tend our garden,
With love and gentle care.
For in these gleeful moments,
We find magic everywhere.

Celebrating Every Step

Every step we take in life,
Deserves a cheer, a shout.
For each small victory won,
Is what life's all about.

Together, hand in hand we tread,
On paths both bright and bold.
With laughter as our compass,
We embrace the stories told.

Through the valleys and the peaks,
We'll dance side by side.
Celebrating every moment,
With hearts open wide.

So raise a glass to progress,
To journeys yet to come.
In each cherished instance,
We will find where we're from.

Streams of Contentment

In streams of gentle waters,
Our minds find sweet repose.
As ripples tell of patience,
In the stillness, peace grows.

The trees sway with soft whispers,
As breezes dance around.
In this land of calm reflections,
True contentment is found.

Floating on these currents,
We find solace and grace.
A tranquil flush of happiness,
In the moment, our pace.

So let us dive in deeply,
To embrace the joy within.
For in these streams of contentment,
Life's beauties shall begin.

Chasing Rainbows

In the sky, colors blend,
After the rain, dreams ascend.
Footsteps light, hearts aglow,
Hoping to find where the treasures flow.

With laughter sweet, we roam free,
Through valleys bright, by the sea.
Each hue whispers tales untold,
Of magic moments, brave and bold.

Chasing visions, young and old,
In every shade, a story unfolds.
Every turn, a twist of fate,
In this journey, love is great.

Hand in hand, we dare to seek,
A pot of gold, a bond unique.
With every step, we learn to grow,
Together we'll chase the vibrant glow.

Navigating to Nirvana

In silence deep, we find our way,
Through tangled thoughts that often sway.
With purpose clear, our paths align,
Towards the light, where spirits shine.

Among the trees, with whispers low,
Nature calls, and we must go.
With open hearts, we seek and trust,
In the stillness, learn to adjust.

Waves of peace wash over the shore,
Guiding us to a world we adore.
In every breath, a moment's grace,
In the quiet, we find our place.

With each step, we shed our fears,
Embracing life, through hopes and tears.
Navigating on this winding road,
To Nirvana, love and dreams bestowed.

A Glimpse of Glee

In morning light, the world awakes,
With laughter bright, the silence breaks.
Children play, their joy runs wide,
In every smile, love resides.

Dancing leaves in a gentle breeze,
Whispers soft among the trees.
A fleeting moment, pure delight,
In simple things, our spirits ignite.

Chasing shadows, laughter flows,
In little joys, our happiness grows.
With hearts open to what may be,
We cherish life, a glimpse of glee.

With every heartbeat, let us sing,
Embracing all the joy we bring.
Together, let our spirits soar,
In the dance of life, forevermore.

Streams of Serenity

A quiet stream flows, crystal clear,
Carving paths where we wander near.
With gentle whispers, nature's hymn,
In every ripple, we learn to swim.

Beneath the shade of ancient trees,
We find moments meant to please.
The world slows down, a soft embrace,
In these still waters, we find our place.

Birds in flight, a tranquil sight,
Guiding us through day and night.
In harmony, our souls entwine,
In streams of peace, we intertwine.

Let the currents carry our dreams,
With every flow, it softly beams.
A tranquil heart, a peaceful mind,
In streams of serenity, bliss we find.

A Tapestry of Cheer

In the morning's gentle light,
Laughter dances, pure and bright.
Colors weave in joyous threads,
Painting life where hope is spread.

Gathered friends in sunny parks,
Sharing stories, leaving marks.
Sunshine spills on soft green grass,
Moments cherished, none shall pass.

Music floats on breezy air,
Each sweet note, a soul laid bare.
Together we embrace the day,
In this tapestry we play.

Whispering Woods of Joy

Beneath the trees where shadows play,
Nature hums a soft ballet.
Birds are singing songs of cheer,
Whispers telling tales so dear.

Leaves flutter like a gentle sigh,
Underneath the vast blue sky.
Every step, a peaceful heart,
In the woods, we find our part.

Sunlight dapples through the leaves,
Each moment, a joy that weaves.
In this quiet, hearts can mend,
Whispering joy, a faithful friend.

Echoes Beneath Bright Skies

Colors burst as daylight breaks,
Every echo, a gift it makes.
Clouds drift softly, dreams take flight,
Beneath the clear, embracing light.

Footsteps on the sand draw lines,
Where the sea and shoreline twines.
Laughter rides the ocean's spray,
Carving memories in the day.

In this space, our spirits soar,
Each moment calling for much more.
Echoes linger, soft and sweet,
In our hearts, the rhythm beats.

The Fountain of Delight

A fountain flows with crystal grace,
Joyful ripples find their place.
Children gather, laughter rings,
In this moment, magic springs.

Water dances in golden rays,
Reflecting love in myriad ways.
Every splash, a spark of glee,
Carrying dreams so wild and free.

As the sun begins to set,
Whispers of joy we won't forget.
The fountain's song, a sweet embrace,
In its depths, our hearts find space.

Sunlit Journeys

Beneath the golden rays they roam,
Paths illuminated, hearts at home.
With every step, new dreams arise,
Bathed in warmth, 'neath endless skies.

Waves of laughter softly blend,
In echoing joy, the road will bend.
Through forests deep and mountains tall,
Each sunlit journey, they heed the call.

They gather moments, rich and rare,
Whispers of journeys linger in air.
Together they chase the fleeting light,
A tapestry woven, bold and bright.

With steadfast hearts and open hands,
They travel to distant, wondrous lands.
In every sunset, horizons gleam,
Sunlit journeys weave a shared dream.

Smiles in the Distance

From afar, a gentle wave,
A spark of joy that hearts can save.
Smiles flicker, like stars at night,
Bringing warmth, igniting light.

In crowded streets, we feel alone,
Yet love's brief glance calls us home.
In every turn, each face we meet,
Smiles in the distance, bittersweet.

Through laughter shared, our spirits soar,
In kindness' arms, we crave for more.
A simple act, a knowing grin,
The warmth inside begins to spin.

So when the world feels cold and grey,
Remember smiles will light the way.
In every moment, near or far,
Smiles in the distance, our guiding star.

The Dance of Serenity

In twilight's glow, the stillness speaks,
A gentle breeze, the soul it seeks.
Soft shadows sway, a tranquil song,
In nature's arms, where hearts belong.

Each leaf that trembles, every sigh,
Calls forth dreams, like birds they fly.
In whispered tones, the world unwinds,
The dance of serenity, where peace finds.

Clear waters mirror the evening hue,
Reflecting hopes, a tranquil view.
With every pulse, the heart will blend,
In rhythmic grace, where worries end.

So close your eyes, let calm descend,
In this sweet dance, may we transcend.
The night unfolds, our spirits free,
In harmony's embrace, we find the key.

Footprints of Light

Each day we travel, paths unknown,
In every step, our seeds are sown.
Footprints of light, where we have been,
Tracing the journey, a sacred sheen.

With every stride, we leave a mark,
In shadows deep, we bring the spark.
Guided by hope, through darkest times,
The rhythm of life in whispered rhymes.

Together we wander, hand in hand,
Creating a map across the land.
In laughter's echoes, our spirits soar,
Footprints of light, forevermore.

So when you tread on paths anew,
Remember the traces, pure and true.
For in each footprint, a story's told,
In the dance of life, both brave and bold.

The Blissful Horizon

Where the sky meets the sea, so bright,
Dreams awaken in morning light.
Waves whisper tales of the day,
Inviting hearts to dance and sway.

Clouds drift lazily, soft and white,
Painting the canvas, a pure delight.
Sunshine spills gold on gentle shores,
Happiness found in endless tours.

Footprints linger in warm, damp sand,
Reminders of joy, both near and grand.
As the tides push and pull away,
New hopes arise with the break of day.

In the distance, horizons gleam,
Each moment alive, a vivid dream.
Together we chase the afternoon,
Under the spell of the sun and moon.

Chasing After Laughter

In the meadows where wildflowers sway,
We toss our cares, let them drift away.
Laughter bubbles like a crystal stream,
Filling the air with a bright, warm gleam.

Chasing shadows in the golden light,
We run like children, hearts taking flight.
Moments shared, joyful and free,
We find our happiness in simple glee.

Echoes of giggles weave through the day,
Reminding us love leads the way.
With each chuckle, the world's less gray,
Together we'll dance, come what may.

Through fields and paths, we stroll with grace,
Chasing after laughter, our joyful chase.
As dusk settles, we'll still hold tight,
To the echoes of joy that light up the night.

Routes of Renewal

Amidst the woods where silence calls,
Nature whispers as the evening falls.
Paths untraveled, fresh and bright,
Lead us onward, towards the light.

With every step, we shed our past,
Finding solace as we breathe and last.
Leaves rustle gently in the breeze,
Healing begins among the trees.

Moments of pause in the cool, sweet air,
Time to reflect, to stop and stare.
Guided by stars in the velvet night,
Routes of renewal feel so right.

Upon this journey, hand in hand,
Together we'll wander, a promised land.
For every path that we choose to take,
Is a stepping stone, a chance to awake.

Sprints of Serenity

In the quiet hours of dawn's embrace,
We find our peace, our sacred space.
With gentle strides, we move along,
Sprinting through silence, where hearts belong.

Breath by breath, with the world in view,
Every heartbeat feels fresh and new.
Moments cherished, swift yet slow,
In sprints of serenity, our spirits grow.

Nature's canvas surrounds us wide,
In every step, we take in the tide.
Rushing waters clear our minds,
In joy and calm, true solace finds.

As day unfolds, we glide with grace,
In every challenge, we embrace the pace.
For in our races, wild and free,
We discover life's sweet harmony.

Milton Keynes UK
Ingram Content Group UK Ltd.
UKHW051811101024
449294UK00007BA/61